Thailand Sketchbook

PORTRAIT OF THE KINGDOM

Paintings © Taveepong Limapornvanich, 2002
Text © William Warren, 2002
Design and typography © Editions Didier Millet, 2002

First published 2002
Reprinted 2008
Paperback edition 2014

Published by
Editions Didier Millet
121 Telok Ayer Street #03-01
Singapore 068590

www.edmbooks.com

Editor: Shan Wolody
Designers: Norreha bte Sayuti and Yolande Lim
Production Manager: Sin Kam Cheong

Colour separation by Singapore Sang Choy Pte Ltd
Printed in Singapore by Tien Wah Press Pte Ltd

ISBN: 978-981-4385-88-6

Printed on 160gsm Modigliani Neve

The publisher wishes to thank the Jim Thompson Foundation for its generous assistance with the launch arrangements for this book.

Artist's Acknowledgements

I have always been interested in different styles of architecture from around the world, which is why I was so enthusiastic to work on this Sketchbook. Particularly when it involved sketching and painting the architecture and landscapes of my homeland.

I would like to express my gratitude to the following people: Shan Wolody, my friendly editor who has kept in touch with me closely whilst keeping an editorial eye on my handwritten captions; my friends Mr Phichit Viwatrujirapong and his wife Mrs Manee Chantarawaranyoo for their never-ending enthusiasm for my work; my friend Mr Erwin Ho, who made my detailed research of Bangkok both convenient and fun; Khun Yuth Jermjutitham, who accompanied me on my many trips to the north and northeast of Thailand; Khun Pattanachai Kulasiriswad, who provided me with transportation and assistance during my research in Bangkok; and finally, my sister Miss Sunisa Limapornvanich, who helped me with my correspondence with the publisher as well as scanning the paintings and numerous computer tasks.

My special thanks go to Mr Nick Mason, who introduced me to the publisher Editions Didier Millet after seeing my paintings in my studio in Phuket.

Words are not enough to express what a wonderful country Thailand is and so it was an honour to be invited by my publisher, Mr Didier Millet, to sketch it.

Finally, I hope that the use of my pencils and brushes will bring enjoyment to the readers of *Thailand Sketchbook*.

Taveepong Limapornvanich
www.taveepong.com

Opposite: A spirit house, dedicated to the guardian spirit of a compound.
Endpapers: Thai mural paintings, executed by anonymous artists in two-dimensional style, nearly always depict religious scenes, such as the life of the Buddha or the Jataka tales, which deal with the Buddha's previous existences. Some also contain vignettes of daily life or episodes from the Thai version of the epic Ramayana.

Thailand Sketchbook

PORTRAIT OF THE KINGDOM

Paintings by Taveepong Limapornvanich

Text by William L. Warren

edm EDITIONS
DIDIER
MILLET

Remains of Wat Mahathat, the largest temple in the ancient capital of Sukhothai.

Contents

Introduction

Sometimes compared in shape to an elephant's head, with its long trunk extending down to Malaysia, Thailand is a kingdom of notable variety in both topography and culture.

The far north, sharing borders with Burma and Laos, is a rugged mountainous region, with elevations that rise to more than 2,500 metres (8,200 feet), cool winter temperatures, and mist-shrouded river valleys. In the northeast, a rolling plateau stretches to the broad Mekong River, while the fertile central plains, one of the world's greatest rice-growing areas, have been the scene of the most intense Thai cultural and economic development. The south, a long narrow peninsula, is flanked by two coastlines, one on the Gulf of Thailand and the other on the Indian Ocean, with picturesque beaches and jungle-clad limestone cliffs.

Due to its central location and natural abundance, the country has been a magnet for human settlement since the dawn of civilisation in Asia. The earliest humans were simple hunter-gatherers, whose Stone-Age remains have been found at several locations. Later, rice-growing communities appeared, as well as others with such sophisticated skills as pottery-making and metal-casting. The most dramatic discoveries have been in the arid northeast, where a somewhat mysterious culture known as Ban Chiang developed some 6,000 years ago; by AD 300, the people of Ban Chiang were producing beautiful pots with swirling red decorations, and refined bronze objects that ranged from weapons to ceremonial items.

Historically, the first arrivals were the Mons, who settled mostly in what is now central and western Thailand between the 9th and 11th centuries. They practised Theravada

Giant guardian figure in the compound of the Temple of the Emerald Buddha in Bangkok.

Sao Hong, a mythological bird, in the Grand Palace, Bangkok.

Aisawan Tippaya Asna Pavilion, a fine example of classic Thai architecture, at the summer palace of Bang Pa - In.

Buddhism, a faith they had acquired from India, and built impressive monuments with superb sculptures and stucco decorations. Their dominance was replaced by the expanding Khmer empire, ruled from the great capital of Angkor, which eventually controlled much of present-day Thailand. Massive stone Khmer temples with finely carved lintels, originally dedicated to Hindu gods but later converted to Buddhism, are scattered throughout the northeastern region, among the most notable being those at Phimai and Phanom Rung.

There is some debate on the subject, but most authorities believe the Thai originated in southern China and gradually migrated down into the present country in search of greater independence and better farmlands. In any event, by the 13th century, when Khmer power was waning, they were sufficiently numerous to establish city-states of their own. One group emerged in the far north, where under King Mengrai they formed a confederation known as Lanna. Another, on the northern edge of the central plains, founded Sukhothai in 1238, traditionally regarded as the first independent Thai kingdom.

Sukhothai's real power lasted less than two centuries, but its cultural contributions loom large over Thai history. Here the Thai script evolved into a definite form and, as majestic ruins still attest, distinctively Thai forms of Buddhist architecture and sculpture were created. Sukhothai Buddha images, particularly the famous Walking Buddha, are notable for their highly stylised elegance and beauty, its temples for their graceful bell-shaped stupas and lotus-bud finials. The kingdom also produced large quantities of fine glazed ceramic wares, which were exported to countries as far away as Indonesia and the Philippines.

Most of all, perhaps, Sukhothai is remembered for its benevolent, paternalistic form of monarchy, very different from the aloof god-kings of the Khmer. These virtues are extolled in a famous stone inscription of 1298, carved during the reign of King

Painted prehistoric pottery from Ban Chiang in the northeast.

Ramkhamhaeng the Great, which contains a famous evocation of the kingdom's freedom and prosperity still learned by all Thai school children: 'This land of Sukhothai is thriving. There are fish in the water and rice in the fields. The lord of the realm does not levy toll on his subjects. They are free to lead their cattle or ride their horses and to engage in trade; whoever wants to trade in elephants, does so; whoever wants to trade in horses, does so; whoever wants to trade in silver and gold, does so.'

Other strong Thai states also emerged, however, and one of them was Ayutthaya, founded in 1350 in the Chao Phraya River basin. From a small fortified island-city situated at the confluence of three rivers, Ayutthaya grew into a mighty kingdom that eventually absorbed Sukhothai and extended over a vast territory that it ruled for most of the next four centuries.

The city itself became one of Asia's most cosmopolitan capitals, filled with hundreds of splendid temples and crisscrossed by man-made waterways that served as streets. Buddhism was the state religion, but the kings ruled with absolute god-like power, only occasionally emerging from their palaces for memorable processions on elephant back or in fleets of carved and gilded barges.

Prasat Hin
Phanom Rung,
a Khmer temple of
the Angkor Wat period,
in Buri Ram Province.

Ayutthaya was often at war, sometimes with the northern Lanna kingdom and with Cambodia but more often with neighbouring Burma. Nevertheless, it was also a thriving commercial entrepôt and attracted many outsiders. Among the earliest arrivals were the Chinese, who came in their huge junks on the annual monsoon winds to exchange silk, porcelain and other luxury goods for such local products as rare woods, animal hides, elephant tusks and edible birds' nests collected in the far south. Muslim merchants came too, from India and further west, as well as Japanese and Persians, some of whom settled in Ayutthaya and became active in Thai affairs.

European traders also made their way up the winding Chao Phraya. The first were the Portuguese, in 1511, who concluded a treaty with Ayutthaya and received permission to settle in the city in return for supplying guns and ammunition to the Thai king. The Spanish came next and, in the following century, the British, the Dutch and the French.

French accounts provide us with the most detailed portrayal of the city at the peak of its power. They arrived during the reign of King Narai (1656-89), the kingdom's most outward-looking ruler, and grand embassies were exchanged between Ayutthaya and the court of Louis XIV. Despite this auspicious beginning, however, relations were short-lived. Attempts by Catholic missionaries to convert King Narai, together with suspicions that the French intended to establish a military foothold in Siam, aroused conservative elements at the court and resulted in a revolt in

The Walking Buddha, one of Sukhothai's greatest artistic creations.

1688. The French were expelled, along with most (though not all) other foreigners living and trading in the capital.

The end of Ayutthaya came in the next century, during a disastrous war with Burma. The city fell in 1767, after which it was sacked and burnt by the enemy, its demoralised and starving population driven into the countryside. Only ruins remain today, though their size and extent still offer haunting testimony to the greatness of the former capital.

Recovery was remarkably swift. A new and vigorous leader emerged in the person of a former provincial governor and military leader who, within a few years, managed to rally troops, defeat the Burmese and set himself up as King Taksin. Because of the total devastation of Ayutthaya, he moved the capital further down the Chao Phraya to the small but strategic town of Thonburi. Here he built a palace near one of several fortresses that had guarded the river approach to Ayutthaya and, over the next 15 years, revived foreign trade while also extending Thai territory and repelling several Burmese attempts at reconquest.

The strain of so much fighting took its toll on the king, however, and following a palace revolt in 1782 he was overthrown and replaced by another noted military leader named Chao Phraya Chakri, founder of the present Chakri Dynasty and known to Thai history as King Rama I.

One of Rama I's first decisions on coming to the throne was to move the capital across the river to a prosperous little trading port called Bangkok. His reasons were partly strategic since the site was more defensible than Thonburi in the event of future invasions. They were also psychological, for he felt his new dynasty should be celebrated with a far grander capital city, one that would in fact rival Ayutthaya's still-remembered splendours.

To this end, he ordered a new canal to be dug at a point where the river curved sharply, thus creating an artificial island similar to that at the heart of the old capital. A community of Chinese traders on the site was moved further downriver, outside the city walls, where it became the nucleus of Bangkok's future Chinatown, after which construction of the Grand Palace began. This took three years and resulted in an extensive compound, nearly 1.6 kilometres (one mile) square, filled with what is still the greatest collection of classic Thai buildings, adorned with multi-tiered roofs and a lavish array of gilded wood-carving, glass mosaic, mother-of-pearl inlay and other decorative details. One corner contained Wat Phra Keo, the royal temple, where the sacred Emerald Buddha was enshrined amid an even greater display of magnificent architecture.

The new capital was given a long, honorific-filled name, shortened by Thais as Krung Thep, 'City of Divinities'; most foreigners, however, have continued to use the name of the village which appeared on so many early maps.

With the fortified island as its core, early Bangkok prospered. As in Ayutthaya, the river and a series of canals served as streets, increasingly crowded with boats that ranged from simple canoes hewn from single logs to elaborate royal barges. The first five Chakri kings were all enthusiastic builders, not only adding new temples but restoring old ones. Wat Phra Chetuphon (Wat Po), the largest in the city as well as the oldest, was transformed during the reign of Rama III into a type of 'open university' with all sorts of educational displays, while Wat Arun, the Temple of Dawn, on the west bank of the river, acquired a cluster of soaring Khmer-style towers decorated with sparkling bits of coloured porcelain.

Ordinary people lived mostly in double, and sometimes triple, rows of wooden floating houses along the river, far simpler than the more solid palaces yet displaying the same steep roofs and elegance of line. Numerous immigrants soon began to arrive from southern China and with them came a taste for Chinese architecture and ornamental features.

European traders and emissaries appeared on the scene during the second and third reigns. A Portuguese merchant named Carlos Manual Silveira was one of the earliest; as he was willing to sell modern weapons, he was warmly received and granted land on which to erect what eventually became the Portuguese Embassy, the oldest in Bangkok. A Scot named Robert Hunter, who arrived shortly after Rama III came to the throne, also succeeded in business and received permission to build one of the first purely Western-style houses on the west bank, an area that was then largely undeveloped.

The most dramatic changes in the city's appearance, though, came under the following two Chakri rulers. Rama IV had spent most of his early life as a Buddhist monk, giving him an unprecedented opportunity to travel around the country and get to know a wide range of people, among them Protestant and Catholic missionaries. He was the first Thai king to have a working knowledge of Latin, French and English, as well as a keen awareness of the dangers confronting his kingdom from the expanding European colonies on all sides. Modernisation, he believed, was the best hope of retaining independence, and he set about achieving it as quickly as possible.

Ruins of Wat Phra Keo at Khamphaeng Phet, in the central plains, an important city during the Sukhothai period.

Three restored chedis at Wat Phra Si Sanphet, the most important temple of Ayutthaya.

An historic treaty with Great Britain, in 1855, led to similar ones with other Western countries and greatly increased the country's trade. More and more foreigners came to Bangkok, some for relatively short stays like Anna Leonowens, whose unreliable memoirs later inspired *The King and I*, others diplomats and businessmen for whom the city became a semi-permanent home. It was at least partly in response to complaints by the latter group that the first real roads were constructed, running near the river in the early days but gradually extending away from it.

Rama V, King Chulalongkorn, not only continued the reforms initiated by his father but broadened them so extensively that almost every aspect of Thai life was transformed during his momentous 42-year reign. He abolished slavery, reorganised provincial administration as well as the armed forces, hired foreign advisers in various government departments, started schools for civil servants and sent nearly all his sons abroad to receive the most modern education. Visually, his influence can still be seen in many parts of Bangkok. Within the Grand Palace compound he replaced many of the older structures with European buildings, most notably the Chakri Maha Prasat, designed by an English architect in a striking mixture of Thai and Western styles. A similar blend, though retaining more classic Thai features, was achieved at Wat Rajabopit and Wat Benchamabopit, both also dating from the fifth reign.

The most dramatic effort at city planning was undertaken in the Dusit District, north of the palace. Rama V made two state visits to Europe and, on his return from the first, conceived a new area along the lines of London and Paris. The focal point

The remains of a bell-shaped chedi, with stucco elephants at its base, at Wat Maheyong, Ayutthaya.

would be a new palace and throne hall, and to reach them he constructed Ratchadamnoen (Royal Progress) Avenue, a broad boulevard reminiscent of the Champs Elysées. Other tree-lined streets were laid out in Dusit, together with parks and handsome buildings set in spacious gardens.

But Bangkok stubbornly insisted on growing in other directions, mostly to the south and southeast, according to its own, less rational, plan. At first the city remained close to the river, where most of the foreign embassies and such buildings as the Oriental Hotel, the East Asiatic Company and the old Customs House were located. Gradually, though, it began to spread inland, following new roads cut through former rice fields and fruit orchards. Chulalongkorn University was built on one of these by Rama VI, who named it after his father; the British

Embassy also moved to another location, described at the time by a disapproving English resident as being 'on the fringes of town'. The first automobile, driven by one of the king's sons, appeared in 1902; six years later, there were 300, and within a remarkably short time Bangkok's dependence on waterways was effectively over, though the Chao Phraya remained an important artery for the transport of goods. The first bridge over the river was opened by King Rama VII in 1932 as one of the events celebrating the 150th anniversary of Bangkok's founding, and formerly isolated Thonburi became more accessible to settlement.

In that same year the centuries-old absolute monarchy came to an end with a bloodless coup d'état led by a small group

Vichai Prasit Fort on the west bank of the Chao Phraya River in Bangkok.

of military officers and civil servants. The king agreed to serve under a constitutional government and Thailand entered a new political age, one symbolised by the Democracy Monument on Ratchadamnoen Avenue.

The kingdom remained largely on the sidelines during World War II and was spared the social disruption suffered by other countries of Southeast Asia. It did not emerge fully unscathed, however. Japanese forces made use of many facilities, including the railways – the infamous Siam-Burma Railway that inspired *The Bridge on the River Kwai* began in Kanchanaburi Province – and parts of Bangkok were bombed in the last year of the war. But its treasured independence was intact, its abundant rice fields still as productive as ever.

In the immediate postwar years, and for some time afterwards, Bangkok looked physically much as it had at the end of Rama V's reign, a city of mostly low-rise buildings and colourful Buddhist temples sprawling in a rather haphazard way over the flat river delta. The highest elevation was Phu Khao Thong, the Golden Mount, a man-made hill topped by a gilded spire that had been started by Rama II and continued under the next three rulers. New areas were developing, but New Road was still the centre for foreign tourists and the majority of business deals originated in the crowded streets of Chinatown. Railways now led to Chiang Mai in the north, eastward to the borders of Laos and Cambodia, and southward to Malaysia; but most provincial regions remained essentially undeveloped.

All this began to change dramatically in the 1960s, not just in Bangkok but in other parts of the country. Modern techniques of construction led to more high-rise structures in the capital,

This statue was erected in memory of King Taksin the Great, who liberated Thailand and established his capital at Thonburi.

creating an impressive new skyline and dozens of different centres within the course of a single generation. An extensive highway system, together with air services, brought even the most remote areas within easy reach of Bangkok and unified the country in a way it had never really been before.

Bangkok remains Thailand's ultimate city, 45 times larger than its nearest rival and the centre of government, monarchy and most leading business firms. For this reason it serves as a powerful magnet to people from provincial areas, most of them young, lured by its varied job opportunities, by its prestigious educational institutions, often merely by its fabled bright lights and endless supply of amusements.

Old view of the Golden Mount, constructed in the mid-19th century and long the highest point in Bangkok.

But prosperity has come to other regions as well. Far northern provinces like Chiang Mai, for example, now have thriving capital cities as well as mountain scenery, cooler weather in the winter and a distinctive culture that draws Thai as well as foreign tourists. The same thing has happened in the south, where tourism has transformed once-empty beaches of idyllic islands such as Phuket and Samui into year-round resorts for visitors from all over the world. Even the northeast, formerly the kingdom's poorest region (and, not coincidentally, the source of most of Bangkok's migrant population), has benefited. With the opening of the first bridge across the Mekong River to Laos, it has become the gateway to Indo-China as well as offering such attractions of its own as Khmer ruins, prehistoric sites, an ancient tradition of silk weaving and a number of colourful local festivals seen nowhere else.

Despite all these changes, Thailand retains the multi-faceted charm that has drawn so many over the years, providing visitors from abroad with a wide range of memorable experiences.

Those who have developed a taste for the subtle flavours of Thai cuisine can sample the real thing and find that each region has its particular specialities. They can also discover that for all its soaring new skyscrapers and gaudy entertainment centres, Bangkok still has areas that evoke the atmosphere of its past: temples of dazzling splendour, markets selling an astonishing assortment of goods and canals that wander through scenes scarcely changed from a century ago.

Elsewhere, they can take an elephant ride through dense forests, visit exotic hill tribe people, see the remains of ancient capitals such as Sukhothai and Ayutthya, or relax on sunstruck beaches of white sand. For nature-lovers, there are some 60 national parks and wildlife preserves, ranging from mountainous to marine.

A diverse kingdom indeed, one with a rich cultural heritage and a still unfolding future of exciting new possibilities.

The bridge on the River Kwai is a reminder of the infamous railway built by prisoners during World War II.

Bangkok

Now sprawling over some 1,540 square kilometres (595 square miles) on both sides of the Chao Phraya River, Bangkok today presents a strikingly modern façade. Air-conditioned shopping centres, lofty skyscrapers and luxury hotels seem to rise everywhere, while traffic roars past on a complex network of elevated expressways. A first-time visitor may feel a certain initial dismay and wonder whatever became of the city described by so many travellers of the past, with its fabulous Buddhist temples and palaces and atmospheric waterways, its colourful markets and traditional Thai ways of life.

But a surprising amount of old Bangkok still survives, sometimes intermingled with its newer additions, sometimes in whole areas that have altered only slightly over the years.

For the greatest concentration of such features, Rattanakosin Island, the original heart of the city, is the best place to start. Here, within high white walls, stands the dazzling Grand Palace and its adjacent Temple of the Emerald Buddha, a fantasy world of gilded spires and multi-coloured roofs that has symbolised the Thai monarchy ever since it was built at the end of the 18th century.

The palace compound covers 25 hectares (61 acres) and, in a series of inter-connected courtyards, contains offices for the royal staff, audience halls, residential quarters and a well-guarded inner area once reserved for the royal wives and their numerous attendants. The imposing Chakri Maha Prasat, built in 1882, is a blend of Western and Thai architecture, but older structures are peerless examples of classical Thai style. Wat Phra Keo, the Temple of the Emerald Buddha, enshrines the most venerated image in the kingdom, whose robes are

Phra Thinang Aphonphimok Prasat, a changing pavilion within the Grand Palace compound.

Emblem of the Chakri Dynasty on the pediment above the entrance to the Chakri Maha Prasat.

The Chakri Maha Prasat in the Grand Palace compound is built in a mixture of Western and Thai architectural styles.

ceremonially changed at the beginning of each of Thailand's three seasons. The decorations, ranging from walls of intricate glass mosaics to gold-and-black lacquer paintings, constitute a virtual textbook of traditional Thai skills.

Also on Rattanakosin Island are such attractions of early Bangkok as Wat Po, with its enormous Reclining Buddha and its school of traditional medicine; Wat Mahathat, a famous centre of Buddhist learning; the National Museum, with a collection that ranges over Thai history; and Lak Muang, the city pillar, where hundreds come every day to offer prayers. Sanam Luang, the great oval field outside the palace, is the traditional setting for royal cremations but also a favourite place for festivals and, at the beginning of the hot season, traditional Thai sports such as kite-fighting.

The nearby Dusit district is full of palatial, colonial-style buildings that became popular towards the end of the 19th century. Among the more notable are Vimarn Mek, an 81-room mansion built entirely of golden teak, and the imposing

The Grand Palace and the Temple of the Emerald Buddha, the greatest display of classic Thai art and architecture, as seen from Sanam Luang.

Ananda Samakhom throne hall which once served as the Thai Parliament.

Chinatown, with its narrow, crowded streets, is another part of Bangkok that has changed little over the years. A highlight here is Sampheng Lane, running for some seven blocks and lined with shops selling everything from gold chains to kitchen equipment. At one end is Pahurat, the cloth market, another longtime favourite with city shoppers.

Still more fascinating glimpses of the past can be found in other older sections of the city. The Golden Mount remains, now over-shadowed by taller buildings but still an impressive elevation with its winding staircase to the summit. In a square across from Wat Suthat, one of Bangkok's most beautiful temples, is the Giant Swing, once the site of a Brahmin festival in which young men mounted on a swing made daring attempts to snatch bags of money suspended from lofty bamboo poles.

Perhaps the most effective way to get the flavour of traditional Bangkok is to forsake the streets and go along the Chao Phraya

River, still an important artery of communication. Old and new co-exist on the river banks: towering condominiums and elegant 19th-century mansions, busy markets and spectacular Buddhist monasteries. The distinctive towers of Wat Arun, the Temple of Dawn, sparkle in the morning sunlight, while not far away is Santa Cruz, a Catholic church dating from 1834. The old Customs House is here, along with the Oriental Hotel, the French Embassy, Vichai Prasit Fortress (near which King Taksin built his Thonburi palace), Pak Klong Talaad (the great cut-flower market) and, at the entrance to Klong Bangkok Yai, a museum housing the royal barges with their ornately carved prows in the shape of mythical birds and beasts.

Along the klongs, or canals, that lead off the river on the Thonburi side, amid fruit and vegetable gardens, people still live in open-fronted wooden houses and still shop from vendor boats selling household goods and a variety of readymade foods.

Even contemporary Bangkok offers serendipitous discoveries and surprises. No shopping centre in the world can compare with the sheer variety of goods on sale at the incredible Weekend Market at Chatuchak Park, just a short distance from the international airport, and the sleek, modern new Sky Train offers not only speedy transportation but also a panorama of unexpected views hidden from ground level. Lumpini Park, an oasis in one of the busiest areas, serves as a recreation centre for city residents, while Siam Square provides a glimpse into youthful lifestyles.

With its blend of legendary past and vibrant present, Bangkok continues to exert a potent spell.

The Memorial Bridge, the first to span
the Chao Phraya River, opened in 1932 to
celebrate Bangkok's 150th anniversary.

The Emerald Buddha
is the most revered of
all the countless
Buddha images
in Thailand.

Wat Phra Keo, the Temple
of the Emerald Buddha, with the Golden Stupa,
the Phra Mondop and a Khmer-style prang.

An entrance to Wat Phra Keo,
viewed from within the enclosure

Mythological creatures from the Temple of the Emerald Buddha. Half human and half animal, these figures are often seen in temple murals.

Apsarasingha

Theppaksi

Thepnorasi

The Golden Mount today, with Wat Saket at the bottom. For many years this was the highest point in Bangkok and most early photographs of the city were taken from its summit.

Wat Rajabopit was constructed during the reign of King Rama V in a mixture of Thai and Western styles.

Chinese figures at Wat Arun. Many of these came in the mid-19th century as ballast on junks returning from the rice trade to China.

Detail of guardian figures supporting
the main tower of Wat Arun, decorated
with pieces of porcelain in stucco.

Wat Arun, the Temple of Dawn,
is one of Bangkok's most famous landmarks.
The central tower rises 81 metres (265 feet).

Chulalongkorn University,
Thailand's oldest, was
established in 1917 by
King Rama VI.

The Democracy Monument on Rachadamnoen
Avenue commemorates the introduction of
constitutional government in 1932.

Thammasat University, founded in 1936 as the University of Moral and Political Sciences.

Garuda, a mythological half-bird, half-human creature, symbolises royalty and authority.

Bangkok 29

One of the numerous courtyards in
Wat Po, Bangkok's largest temple.

The Reclining Buddha at Wat Po is 46 metres
(150 feet) long. The soles of the feet are
inlaid with beautiful mother-of-pearl
designs showing the 108 marks by which
the true Buddha can be recognised.

The viharn, or assembly building, at Wat Suthat, one of Bangkok's most beautiful monasteries.

The Giant Swing (Sao Chin Cha) opposite Wat Suthat, was once the focus of an annual Brahmin festival.

A singha, or mythical lion, guarding the entrance to Wat Benchamabopit.

Thailand's largest bronze bell, at Wat Kalayanimit on the Chao Phraya River.

Wat Benchamabopit was constructed
by King Rama V in 1899. The walls
are covered with Carrara marble
from Italy.

The Suphanahongsa, the principal royal barge in which the King rides in processions. It is made from a single teakwood trunk and its graceful prow represents the hamsa, a mythological bird.

Floral wreath and pendant around the neck of the hamsa at the prow of the Suphanahongsa.

The Narai Songsubhond,
newest of the royal barges,
was presented to the King
on the occasion of his
Golden Jubilee in 1996.

Bangkok 35

Klong Bangkok Noi in Thonburi, a
scene scarcely changed over the years.
Life in early Bangkok, as in the old capital
of Ayutthaya, was centred on water. Leading from
the main river was a complex network of klongs, or canals,
lined with open-fronted houses and filled with boats of all kinds.

Vendor boats selling produce at the
floating market at Taling chan.

Today's most active floating market is at Damnern Saduak, where hundreds of vendors gather every morning.

The beautiful dome
of Santa Cruz Cathedral.

A statue of Jesus Christ in front of the
Santa Cruz Cathedral, a river landmark.

Santa Cruz Cathedral
on the Chao Phraya River
was first established in early
Bangkok. The present church
dates from 1913.

The landing stage at Santa Cruz is decorated with Victorian fretwork.

Rachinee Landing is one of the busiest along the river in Bangkok. It provides access to Pak Klong Talaad, the wholesale market for flowers and vegetables, and to the commercial district.

Wheel of the Law, one of the basic emblems of Buddhism.

Spirit house at the Jim Thompson house. Daily offerings of flowers and incense are made to the guardian spirit.

A Krathong is set adrift on water to pay homage to the water spirits at the end of the rainy season.

Gigantic statue of the Sukhothai Walking Buddha at Buddha Monthon.

The Erawan Shrine, dedicated to the god Brahma, is one of the most popular non-Buddhist shrines in Bangkok.

Contributing to the construction or restoration of a Buddhist monastery is an important way of earning merit.

Offering food to monks is a daily ritual in which merit is earned.

Siam Square, a popular gathering place for young people with its numerous shops and theatres.

The Sky Train, Bangkok's first mass rapid transit system, opened in 1999.

Lumpini Park in central Bangkok is a favourite place for exercising – tai chi, jogging, body building – as well as public concerts.

Statue of King Rama VI at the entrance to Lumpini Park.

Chinese-style pagoda in Lumpini Park.

Pak Klong Talaad is the city's principal wholesale market for vegetables and cut flowers.

Monument at Rama IX Park, opened on the occasion of the present King's 60th birthday.

With thousands of stalls, the Chatuchak Weekend Market offers almost everything grown or made in Thailand. This is one of the busiest places in Bangkok.

Hua Lamphong,
Bangkok's principal railway
station, was built over a century ago.

The neo-classical Ministry of Defence
building was constructed in the
reign of King Rama V near the
Grand Palace, and is one of Bangkok's
early Western-style buildings.

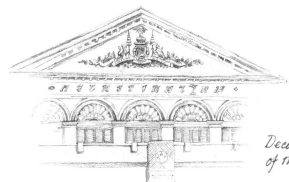

Decorated pediment and arched windows
of the Ministry of Defence.

An equestrian statue of King Rama V stands in front of the Ananda Samakhom Throne Hall and is the focus of many ceremonies honouring the beloved king.

Ananda Samakhom Throne Hall was built as part of the Dusit Palace complex and later used for the National Parliament. King Rama V had intended it to be the centrepiece of his largely Western-style Dusit district.

Detail from the
entrance gate of the
Ananda Samakhom
Throne Hall.

Spiral wooden staircase
in Vimarn Mek.

Vimarn Mek Palace, built entirely of golden teakwood. Erected during
the reign of King Rama V, it was restored by the present Queen as part
of Bangkok's bicentennial celebrations.

A lakeside pavilion in the Vimarn Mek palace grounds is adorned with Victorian fretwork.

Wooden fretwork on the
Aphisek Dusit Palace
audience hall.

Nineteenth-century furnishings
adorn the audience hall.

Located in the grounds of Vimarn Mek, the Aphisek Dusit Palace is now used to display contemporary Thai crafts.

Bangkok 53

Saranrom Palace, used as a residence for Crown Prince Vajiravudh, the future Rama VI, and later by the Ministry of Foreign Affairs.

The windows at
Bangkhunprom
Palace have elaborate
stucco decorations.

Bangkhunprom
Palace, designed
by a German
architect, was the
residence of a Thai
prince and is
currently part of
the Bank of Thailand.

Ho Withun Thasana, an observatory built by King Rama V
at the summer palace of Bang Pa-In,
once a popular royal retreat.

Thewarat Khanlai Gate at Bang Pa-In.

Royal emblem of
King Rama VI on
Boromphiman
Mansion.

Boromphiman Mansion, a Western-style building
in the Grand Palace, has served as the residence for
several Chakri Kings, and is now used for distinguished
foreign state visitors.

Beneharong bowl in Jim Thompson's collection. Beneharong, literally meaning "five colours", is a type of glazed enamelware made in China in the 17th century specifically for export to Thailand.

The Thai-style house of Jim Thompson, the American who revived the Thai silk industry, is now a museum open to the public.

Decorative wooden bells in the lobby of the Oriental Hotel.

The Oriental Hotel's shuttle boat crosses the river to the hotel's Thai restaurant and spa on the West bank.

The Author's Wing of the Oriental Hotel, built in 1887 and the oldest part of Bangkok's most famous hotel.

ศาลา-เฉลิม-กรุง

A royal carriage displayed in the National Museum.

Sala Chaloem Krung, one of Bangkok's oldest cinemas.

This pavilion in the National Museum was once the palace of the Second King, a position that no longer exists.

The shophouses along Thanon Atsadang, near Klong lod, are some of the oldest in Bangkok, most of them built during the reign of King Rama V in the colonial style popular at that time.

Neng Noi Yee Temple, one of the oldest Chinese temples in Bangkok's Chinatown.

Dragons on the Neng Noi Yee Temple roof guard the temple against harm from outside sources.

Chinatown.
Roughly located between Charoen Krung Road and the river, This crowded area has been the heart of Chinese life since early Bangkok.

Sampheng Lane. This narrow covered lane, which runs for seven blocks, is lined with shops selling all kinds of goods, from gold jewellery to wedding souvenirs.

The Tang To Kang gold shop is in a shophouse built in 1872.

Bangkok's oldest pawnshop is in a National Heritage building on Charoen Krung Road.

Many calligraphers still ply their ancient art in Chinatown, especially at Chinese New Year when red-and-gold banners are displayed outside shops.

The North

Funeral chedis of Chiang Mai's royal family at Wat Suan Dok in Chiang Mai.

Northern and northeastern Thailand, sharing borders with Burma, Laos and Cambodia, has long been a world apart. The remote northeast covers one-third of the country yet remains the least known of Thailand's regions, despite its natural and archaeological attractions. In the north, isolated from the central plains by a range of high mountains, a unique Thai culture rose in the late 13th century when several small city-states united to establish Lanna, 'Land of a Million Rice Fields'. Its capital was Chiang Mai, founded by King Mengrai in 1296.

After two centuries, the Lanna kingdom began to decline, though not before developing its own distinctive style. It came under Burmese rule for a long period, adding another cultural flavour, before the Bangkok government took over direct administrative control in the 19th century. Even then it remained remote until the northern railway was opened in 1920.

Chiang Mai has expanded greatly over recent years, but it still has a remarkable number of elegant Buddhist temples as well as a large population of artisans skilled in such crafts as woodcarving, lacquerware, silk weaving, silverware and handmade paper. Lamphun, even older, was a centre of Mon culture as long ago as the 9th century. Fine old wooden houses, elaborately adorned with Victorian fretwork, can be seen in Lampang, once the centre of the teak industry when countless huge logs were floated down rivers and eventually to sawmills in Bangkok. Adding to the region's cultural blend are various tribal people, who live at higher elevations and continue to follow their own traditional ways.

A century ago an Englishman described the north as 'an Asian Arcady'. Visitors are still enchanted by its special qualities.

Wat Phra That Doi Suthep, one of the most revered temples in northern Thailand, is near the top of the mountain which overlooks Chiang Mai. Ringing the temple's bells (above) is believed to bring good luck.

Phra Thamnak Doi Tung in Chiang Rai Province once served as a residence for the mother of the present King.

Thaphae Gate, one of the entrances to the old walled city of Chiang Mai.

ประตูท่าแพ
ปจว.ชร.๔๔๓
THA PHAE GATE

Boonma House in Lampang is today
used as a guesthouse. The V-shaped decorations
at the end of the roof beams, called kalae, are
typical of northern houses.

A skilled
tradesman works
on the restoration
of a teakwood
bridge.

Stucco standing deities
are among the beautiful
decorations on Wat
Ched Yod, Chiang Mai,
built in 1455 by King
Tilokaraja whose
ashes are enshrined
there.

The village of Bo Sang, ten kilometres (six miles) from
Chiang Mai, is almost entirely devoted to the making
of colourful umbrellas, some of cloth but most of
oiled rice paper painted with floral designs.

The viharn, or assembly hall, of Wat Phra Singh
was built around 1806 and is a classic
example of Lanna architecture.
The temple itself was founded
in 1345.

Nagas, or sacred
serpents, serve
as guardian
figures at the
foot of staircases
in many temples,
especially in
the north.

Old market houses in Lampang
mostly date from a century ago
when the province was a centre
of the teak industry.

Ban Sao Nak, "the house of many pillars," was built in 1885 by a Burmese merchant who settled in Lampang.

Horse-drawn carts are a leisurely way to explore the streets of Lampang.

Young elephants being trained at the Elephant Conservation Centre, Lampang.

Elephants at work in the northern teak forests, pulling huge logs to riverbanks to be floated down to sawmills.

The largest gong in the world at Wat Phra That Haripunchai in Lamphun, an ancient city founded by Mon people.

Northern artisans have long been famous for their fine pottery, especially celadon, which is still produced by traditional methods.

A richly ornamented
Burmese-style building
with a graceful tiered
roof stands in the
compound of Wat
Phra Keo Don Tao
in Lampang.

Phra Buddha Chinaraj.
Enshrined at Wat Mahathat
in Phitsanulok Province,
this renowned image of
polished bronze dates from
the 14th century. Many
copies have been made for
other Thai temples, the
most famous being at Wat
Benchamabopit in
Bangkok.

Seated Buddha image in the ruins of
Wat Mahathat in the ancient
capital of Sukhothai.

The North 77

Wat Phra That Phanom, a
Buddhist pilgrimage centre
and the most famous temple
in northeastern Thailand,
overlooks the Mekong River.

The Candle Festival in Ubon
Ratchathani marks the beginning
of the Buddhist period of fasting.
Huge candles and beautiful wax
carvings are paraded around
the town.

Stone lintel on Prasat Phanom Rung, Buri Ram.
This superb example of 12 th - century
Khmer bas - relief carving, showing the Hindu
god Vishnu, was stolen in the early 1960s
and later returned.

Prasat Muang Tham,
a 10 th - century Khmer sanctuary
in Buri Ram Province
near the Cambodian
border.

The South

Reaching down to Malaysia like a long, slender arm, southern Thailand is both visually and culturally different from other regions. A chain of jungle-clad limestone mountains runs along its spine, creating dramatic scenery in places where they spill down into the turquoise seas along both coasts. People derive a livelihood not only from these abundant waters but also from vast plantations of rubber trees and graceful coconut palms, which thrive in the south's long rainy season.

Most of Thailand's two million Muslims live in the southernmost provinces of Narathiwat, Pattani, Yala and Satun, where their domed mosques are as much a part of the landscape as the Buddhist temples are elsewhere. Nakhon Si Thammarat, on the other hand, was a major centre of Theravada Buddhism in the Sukhothai period during the 13th century.

The south also has a distinctive cuisine, with coconut milk, locally grown fruit and seafood playing prominent roles.

For modern tourists, the region's greatest allure lies in its pristine beaches, some on the mainland coast but others, even more enticing, on islands scattered just offshore in both the Gulf of Thailand and the Andaman Sea. Phuket is perhaps the best known of these today, but it can also look back on an eventful history that stretches back to ancient times. Traders came from China and India in search of tin ore, available on the island in large quantities, as well as other treasures like ambergris, rare corals and edible birds' nests harvested in limestone caves. Phuket was thus already a wealthy place, with handsome mansions in the Sino-Portuguese style, long before the first adventurous Western travellers discovered its string of breathtakingly beautiful beaches and made it internationally famous.

The Heroines' monument in Phuket commemorates Thao Thep Kasattri, the wife of the governor of Thalang, and her sister Thao Si Sunthon, who repelled a Burmese invasion in 1785.

Royal Railway Station, at Hua Hin on the Gulf of Thailand, was designed by an Italian architect.

Bronze image of the Bodhisattva from Chaiya,
now in the National Museum in Bangkok,
dates from the 8-9th centuries.

Entrance to one of the
Sino-Portuguese mansions
built by wealthy Chinese
who came to Phuket in
the 19th century.

Wat Phra Boromathat in Chaiya
is one of the reminders of the somewhat
mysterious Srivijaya kingdom.

Old colonial-style shophouses along Deebuk Road in Phuket Town, the provincial capital.

The Villa Royale is a private Phuket home designed by M.L. Tri Devakul overlooking the Andaman Sea.

Living room of M.L. Tri's villa with a modernistic sculpture created by the owner.

This mermaid statue, overlooking popular Samila beach near Songkhla, was installed some time after World War II and appears in many tourist photographs.

Thamnak Khao Noi, the residence of the Governor of Songkhla Province.

Old Chinese-style houses on Nakorn Nai Road in Songkhla, a port known to ancient traders as Singora.

Phra Buddha Taksin Ming Mongkhol, the tallest seated Buddha in Thailand, was erected in 1966 in Narathiwat Province and dominates the landscape.

Koh Tapu, "Nail Island", is one of hundreds of dramatic limestone outcrops in beautiful Phangnga Bay. The odd shapes give rise to a variety of popular names.

Traditional southern fishing boats have elegantly curved and raised prows and are often adorned with colourful painted designs.

A craftsman produces small shadow play puppets from cowhide in Pattalung Province.

Yaksa, or guardian figure, on the wall of Wat Machi Mawat in Songkhla.

Part of the old city wall in Nakhon Si Thammarat, one of the most ancient cities in Thailand.

Wat Machi Mawat includes beautiful murals from the early 19th century.

Wat Phra Mahathat in Nakhon Si Thammarat, with its dominant stupa, probably dates from the early 13th century.

ขอต้อนรับด้วยความยินดียิ่ง
WELCOME TO NARATHIWAS
SELAMAT   DATANG

A sign on the
Thai - Malaysian border
welcomes visitors to
Narathiwat Province.

The elegantly proportioned
Pattani Central Mosque.

Central Mosque in Narathiwat. Muslims
constitute Thailand's largest religious minority
and are concentrated in the far southern provinces.

Gazetteer

INTRODUCTION

Page 7
Aisawan Tippaya Asna Pavilion, Bang Pa-In
Dating from 1876, this Thai-style pavilion has multi-level tiled roofs and contains a bronze statue of King Chulalongkorn. It is set in the middle of a lake at the largely European-style summer palace on the Chao Phraya River near the old capital of Ayutthaya, which was a popular retreat for the king and members of his court. It is considered one of the finest examples of classic Thai architecture and models of it have been used at several international expositions.

Page 8
Prasat Hin Phimai
Located near the northeastern city of Nakhon Ratchasima, this is an 11th-century Khmer temple built of white and pink sandstone during the period when much of Thailand was part of the Khmer Empire. A direct road from the fortified town of Phimai once led to Angkor. One of the best examples of Khmer architecture in Thailand, the temple was restored by the Fine Arts Department in cooperation with Bernard Groslier, a former director of restoration at Angkor.

Page 9
Prasat Hin Phanom Rung, Buri Ram Province
Dating from the 12th century, at the beginning of the Angkor Wat period, this temple is built of sandstone and laterite on an east-west alignment and displays some of the finest Khmer friezes and lintels to be seen in Thailand. It has been beautifully restored by the Fine Arts Department with advice from French experts.

Page 11
Wat Phra Keo, Khamphaeng Phet
Kamphaeng Phet was one of the centres of the Sukhothai kingdom. Among its ruins is Wat Phra Keo, where several seated Buddha images and a reclining image can be seen along with the remains of laterite columns that once supported the main sanctuary.

Page 12
Wat Phra Si Sanphet, Ayutthaya
Founded in the 15th century by King Baroma Trai Lokanat, this served as Ayutthaya's royal temple and was located just south of the palace. The compound contained many bell-shaped chedis built of brick and stucco, the three largest of which have been frequently restored and are among the most famous attractions in the old capital.

Page 13
Wat Maheyong, Ayutthaya
Dating from the late Ayutthaya period, this temple is noted for its elaborate stucco decorations, especially elephants which support the large main chedi and were obviously inspired by similar ones in Sukhothai.

Page 14
Vichai Prasit Fort, Bangkok
During the Ayutthaya period, this and a number of other forts were constructed on the Chao Phraya River at Bangkok to protect the capital against invasions, several of them by French soldiers who came in the late 17th century. King Taksin built his palace within the compound of Vichai Prasit Fort on the west bank at the beginning of the Thonburi period, using the adjacent Wat Arun as the royal temple.

Page 17
Bridge on the River Kwai, Kanchanaburi Province
Located southwest of Bangkok, this much-reconstructed bridge serves as a reminder of the notorious "death railway" built by prisoners of the Japanese in 1942-43 to transport soldiers and supplies between Thailand and Burma. Some 12,000 Europeans and a far greater number of Asian labourers died during the operation. An annual sound-and-light festival is held at the bridge in November.

BANGKOK

Page 18
Phra Thinang Aphonphimok Prasat, Grand Palace
This pavilion in classical Thai style was built by King Rama IV on the east wall which surrounds the Dusit Maha Prasat Throne Hall in the Grand Palace compound. Designed in the form of a modified Greek cross with the short wings on the east and west and crowned by a five-tiered spiral top, it was used as a changing pavilion by the King before he descended a short flight of steps to mount his palanquin.

Page 19
Chakri Maha Prasat, Grand Palace
Designed in neo-classical style by John Clunish, an English architect, this was originally planned as a domed structure, wholly European in appearance. Halfway through construction, however, King Rama V decided to replace the domes with three Thai-style spires to harmonise with the older, traditional structures in the palace compound. Completed in 1882, it contains an audience hall, reception rooms and residential quarters.

Pages 20-21
The Grand Palace Enclosure
Built by King Rama I in 1782-85, the Grand Palace enclosure faces north and originally covered an area of about 21.4 hectares (52.8 acres); another 3.3 hectares (8.2 acres) were added by Rama II in 1809. In addition to an outer area for royal offices, it contains audience halls, residential quarters, and an inner area once reserved for female members of the royal family; Wat Phra Keo, the Temple of the Emerald Buddha, occupies the far right-hand section.

Pages 22-23
Memorial Bridge
This bridge, known in Thai as Saphan Phut, was the first to span the Chao Phraya River, linking Bangkok with Thonburi. It was opened by King Rama VII on April 6, 1932, the 150th anniversary of the Chakri Dynasty. Seven bridges now span the river.

Page 24
Wat Phra Keo, Grand Palace
The Temple of the Emerald Buddha, part of the Grand Palace enclosure, was built by King Rama I and has been added to and refurbished by most of the Chakri Dynasty rulers. The Golden Stupa, for example was constructed by Rama IV and was modelled after one at the royal chapel in Ayutthaya. The architecture and decorations of the complex are considered a virtual textbook of the finest of classical Thai arts.

The Emerald Buddha
According to legend, this relatively small image – 66 centimetres (26 inches) from base to top – of semi-precious nephrite was discovered when lightning struck a stupa in the northern province of Chiang Rai in the early 15th century. It was enshrined in several northern temples before being taken to Vientiane, in Laos, in 1552, where it remained until the founder of the Chakri Dynasty brought it back to Thailand and made it the most revered image of his new capital. Its ornamental robes are changed three times annually, at the beginning of the hot, rainy and cool seasons.

Page 25
The Golden Mount (also shown on page 16)
Construction of the Golden Mount, or Phu Khao Thong, began during the early-19th-century reign of Rama III but due to the technical problems of building such a large structure on muddy soil it was not completed until the reign of Rama V. It is part of Wat Saket, built by Rama I.

Page 26
Wat Rajabopit
This temple was constructed by King Rama V in 1863. The basic inspiration was the great Phra Pathom Chedi in Nakhon Pathom, but a number of Western influences can be seen in its circular cloister and several chapels in Italian Gothic style. In an adjacent enclosure is a group of marble memorials to members of the Chakri family.

Devakul, contains exhibits highlighting various aspects of the King's reign.

Page 45
Chatuchak Weekend Market
Held on Saturday and Sunday, this is Bangkok's largest open-air market and contains some 5,000 stalls selling almost everything produced in Thailand. It is divided into various areas specialising in such items as plants, pets, food, clothing, household goods, antiques, books and many others.

Page 46
Hua Lamphong Station
The principal railway station in Bangkok, this was built over a century ago and modelled after a terminal in Manchester, England. The first line, opened to traffic in 1900, linked the capital with Nakhon Ratchasima, a distance of 306 kilometres (190 miles); a second, opened in 1903, went to Petchaburi on the west coast of the Gulf of Thailand.

Page 47
Ministry of Defence
Construction of this huge building near the Grand Palace started in 1882 and was completed in 1884 on land formerly occupied by three palaces dating from the reign of Rama I. Built in neo-classical style, it was first used as a storehouse and for barracks, but later became the Ministry of Defence.

Page 48
Equestrian Statue of King Rama V
Standing in the square in front of the Ananda Samakhom Throne Hall, this was modelled by a French sculptor, Georges Saulo, when King Rama V visited Paris. It was cast in parts, assembled in Bangkok, and unveiled on November 11, 1908, the 40th anniversary of his coronation. Special ceremonies are held at the statue on October 23, the anniversary of his death, when dignitaries and large numbers of ordinary people come to pay homage to this beloved monarch.

Page 49
Ananda Samakhom Throne Hall
Construction of this imposing building began in 1907, directed by a group of Italian architects and engineers – among them Annibale Rigotti, Carlo Allegri, E.G. Gollo and M. Tamagno – in a combination of neo-classical and Renaissance styles. It was completed five years later, after the death of King Rama V. Galileo Chini, an Italian artist the king had admired, was commissioned to decorate the interior with murals of notable events in Thai history in 1911-13. For a time following the end of the absolute monarchy in 1932, it served as the National Parliament.

Page 50
Vimarn Mek Palace
Built entirely of golden teak, this 81-room Western-style mansion was originally intended to serve as a royal residence on the island of Si Chang in the Gulf of Thailand. Due to conflicts with the French over nearby Cambodia, however, it was decided to move the structure to the Dusit district of Bangkok in 1901. King Rama V lived in it while supervising the construction of Dusit Palace. The palace fell into disrepair after being abandoned in 1935 but was splendidly restored at the request of Queen Sirikit as part of Bangkok's bicentennial celebrations in 1982.

Page 51
Lakeside Pavilion, Vimarn Mek Palace
Ornate Victorian fretwork, popular during the reign of Rama V, was lavishly employed on this and other buildings in the large Vimarn Mek Palace compound.

Pages 52-53
Aphisek Dusit Palace Audience Hall
Adorned with Victorian fretwork, this is part of the Vimarn Mek compound and was used for royal audiences by King Rama V. Today it serves as a showcase for products made by SUPPORT, a foundation established by Queen Sirikit to promote traditional handicrafts as a means of earning supplementary income for villagers in rural areas.

Page 54
Saranrom Palace
Located in spacious grounds east of the Grand Palace, this Western-style palace was built in the late 19th century and for six years, from 1904 to 1910, served as the residence of Crown Prince Vajiravudh before he came to the throne as King Rama VI. It later became the Ministry of Foreign Affairs.

Page 55
Bangkhunprom Palace
Karl Dohring, a German architect, built this palace for Prince Paribatra Sukhumbhand shortly before the death of the prince's father, King Rama V, in 1910. It displays a blend of Renaissance, Baroque, Rococo, and Art Nouveau architectural styles, all of which were popular in Bangkok at the time. After the end of the absolute monarchy in 1932 it was taken over by the government and was used for a variety of purposes until it became the headquarters of the Bank of Thailand in 1945. In the early 1990s, the Bank commissioned a complete renovation, also incorporating a museum of Thai currency.

Page 56
Ho Withun Thasana, Bang Pa-In
This tower, popularly known as the Sage's Lookout, was built at Bang Pa-In summer palace by King Rama V in 1881 and was used for viewing the surrounding countryside.

Thewarat Khanlai Gate, Bang Pa-In
Located on the Chao Phraya River near the old capital of Ayutthaya, Bang Pa-In palace was a popular retreat for the royal court during the reign of King Rama V. It contains buildings in a variety of architectural styles, ranging from Western to Chinese, as well as lakes and waterways. The Thewarat Khanlai Gate, in neo-classical style, has three arched entrances under a balustraded entablature.

Page 57
Boromphiman Mansion
Located within the Grand Palace compound this Renaissance neo-classical mansion with a mansard slate-tiled roof was designed by a German architect and built during the reign of King Rama V as a residence for Crown Prince Vajiravudh. During the Sixth Reign, extensive additions were made, including a glass skylight. It served as the temporary residence of Kings Rama VI, Rama VII, Rama VIII and the present King and is used today to house visiting heads of state.

Page 58
Jim Thompson House
Jim Thompson was an American who arrived in Thailand with the military at the end of World War II and stayed on to revive the Thai silk industry, which he made world famous. In 1959, he also assembled six old traditional Thai houses on Klong Mahanag to serve as a residence and also to display his large collection of art from Thailand and other Asian cultures. Thompson mysteriously disappeared in 1967, but the house is open to the public.

Page 59
The Oriental Hotel
Designed by an Italian architectural firm called Cardu and Rossi, the Oriental Hotel opened on May 14, 1887, with "forty commodious and well furnished rooms." It was owned by H.N. Andersen, founder of the East Asiatic Company, and immediately became Bangkok's best-known hotel. Over the years it has undergone many changes, including the addition of two high-rise wings; the only part of the original that remains is the Author's Wing, crowned by a pediment displaying a golden rising sun.

Page 60
Sala Chaloem Krung
One of the oldest cinemas in Bangkok, located near Chinatown, this was recently restored and is often used for performances attended by members of the royal family.

National Museum
Part of this extensive museum at Sanam Luang is housed in what was once the palace of the Second King, a sort of vice-ruler, and dates from the founding of Bangkok. The office was allowed to lapse during the reign of King Rama V, who donated the palace for the display of the country's artistic heritage. The old buildings include a chapel called Wat Buddhaisawan and extensive residential quarters in which many royal items are displayed, ranging from carriages and elephant howdahs to puppets and dance masks.

Page 62
Neng Noi Yee Temple
This Mahayana Buddhist temple, also known as Wat Mangkon Kamalawat, is located on Charoen Krung Road (New Road) and is one of the oldest Chinese temples in Bangkok. In addition to statues in the Chinese style, it contains a large collection of gilded Rattanakosin Buddha images.

Page 64
Tang To Kang Gold Shop
Built in 1872 at the corner of Soi Vanich and Mangkon Road, this elegant shophouse was typical of many in Bangkok during the reign of Rama V. The Garuda emblem above the entrance indicates that the business has received royal favour.

Page 65
Pawnshop
Located in Chinatown on Charoen Krung Road, this is Bangkok's oldest pawnshop and one of the very few shophouses on the National Heritage list of protected buildings.

THE NORTH

Page 66
Wat Suan Dok, Chiang Mai
Dating from the end of the 14th century, Wat Suan Dok (the Flower Garden Temple) was built by King Ku Na to honour a revered monk who had come from Sri Lanka to teach and supposedly lived in the garden. In addition to a huge bell-shaped chedi, the temple compound also includes a complex of structures containing the remains of Chiang Mai's royal family.

Page 67
Wat Phra That Doi Suthep, Chiang Mai
Located near the top of Doi Suthep, a 1,600-metre (5,250-foot) mountain that overlooks Chiang Mai, this is one of the most revered temples in northern Thailand. It was founded in the 14th century but has been restored and added to extensively over the years since. The gold-plated central chedi, built in the 16th century over an older structure, enshrines relics of the Buddha.

Page 68
Phra Thamnak Doi Tung, Chiang Rai
Built on the mountain of Doi Tung, this served as a northern residence for the mother of the present King and has become a popular tourist destination, famous for its extensive gardens of temperate-zone plants.

Thaphae Gate, Chiang Mai
This is a modern restoration of one of the major gates that once led into the walled city of Chiang Mai.

Page 69
Boonma House, Lampang
Built in 1913, this is a fine example of the typical Lanna house. The V-shaped decorations at the end of the roof beams are known as kalae and are distinctive features on northern-style houses. Lampang, where this is located, was a centre of the teak industry in the late 19th and early 20th centuries .

Page 71
Wat Phra Singh, Chiang Mai
One of the most important temples in Chiang Mai, this was founded in 1345 by King Pha Yu of the Mengrai Dynasty. The Viharn Laikam, in typical northern style, was built around 1806 and houses the famous Phra Buddha Singh, an early bronze Lanna image brought from Chiang Rai in 1400.

Page 72
Houses in the Old Market, Lampang
Usually built in Western style with Chinese and Burmese features, these wooden buildings are reminders of the time, a century ago, when Lampang was a prosperous centre of the teak industry. The elaborate Victorian fretwork was mostly carved by Burmese artisans who came to work in the forests.

Page 73
Ban Sao Nak, Lampang
Built in 1885 by a Burmese who settled in Lampang, this house displays both Burmese and northern Thai architectural styles. The name, which means "the house of many pillars," refers to the fact that it is raised from the ground on 116 stout teak pillars; an old rice granary in the same compound is supported by 24 pillars. The house is now a museum of northern handicrafts.

Page 75
Wat Phra That Haripunchai, Lamphun
What is reputedly the largest gong in the world is on display at this temple in Lamphun, an ancient city founded by Mon people in the 7th century. Wat Phra That Haripunchai, one of the most famous in the city, was established in 1044.

Page 76
Wat Phra Keo Don Tao, Lampang
Located within the compound of a temple that supposedly once enshrined the famous Emerald Buddha, this elaborately decorated Burmese-style structure was built in 1909 as a donation by a Thai prince.

Page 77
Wat Mahathat, Sukhothai (also shown on page 4)
The largest temple in the old capital of Sukhothai, Wat Mahathat covered an area 200 metres by 200 metres (655 feet by 655 feet), surrounded by a moat. The seated Buddha shown here, on a brick foundation, has been restored and dates from the 14th century.

Page 78
Wat Phra That Phanom, Nakhon Phanom
Overlooking the Mekong River, this is the most famous Buddhist temple in the northeast. The original chedi, built in the 9th century, was modelled after the famous That Luang in Vientiane, Laos. When it collapsed during a storm in 1975, it was immediately reconstructed and re-opened four years later by the King.

Page 79
Lintel on Prasat Phanom Rung, Buri Ram
This superb example of Khmer bas-relief carving in sandstone dates from the 12th century and shows the Hindu god Vishnu. It was stolen in the early 1960s and later appeared in the Chicago Art Museum. It was returned to Thailand some 20 years later.

Prasat Muang Tham, Buri Ram
This Khmer sanctuary, richly decorated with carvings of Hindu deities, was built in the second half of the 10th century when northeastern Thailand was part of the great empire ruled from Angkor. It consists of an outer and inner courtyard surrounded by a laterite wall.

THE SOUTH

Pages 80-81
Royal Railway Station, Hua Hin
Soon after the southern railway line reached Hua Hin in 1911, the small fishing village became a popular summer retreat for members of the Thai aristocracy. The station shown here, built in a blend of Thai and Western styles by an Italian architect, was for the exclusive use of the King, who had a palace on the beach.

Page 82

Wat Phra Boromathat, Chaiya

This is the most important monument dating from the Srivijaya period (8th–12th centuries) though it has been restored so often that only the foundations of the original remain. The central prang was restored during the reign of King Rama V and is strikingly Javanese in appearance.

Sino-Portuguese Mansion, Phuket

Many Chinese who came to Phuket in the 19th century made fortunes on the island's rich tin deposits and built mansions like this one on Deebuk Road in Phuket Town. Combining Western and Chinese styles, they resemble those built earlier in Malacca and Penang.

Page 83

Deebuk Road, Phuket

Most of the old, colonial-style shophouses of Phuket Town – two-storey and highlighted with stucco and wood carving – have been torn down to make way for modern structures; but a few still remain, such as these on the corner of Deebuk Road and Yaowarat Road.

Page 84

Villa Royale, Phuket

Designed by prominent architect and developer M.L. Tri Devakul, this private home has been converted into five luxurious suites available to visitors amid a spacious tropical garden on a hill overlooking the sea between Kata Noi and Kata Yai beaches.

Page 85

Thamnak Khao Noi, Songkhla

Built in the reign of Rama V, this handsome colonial-style building now serves as the residence of the Governor of Songkhla Province.

Old Chinese Houses, Nakorn Nai Road, Songkhla

Songkhla, once known as Singora and the only natural port on the lower Gulf of Thailand, was long a prosperous trading centre largely developed by Chinese. Much of the trade eventually moved to Haadyai, on the southern railway, but many fine old Chinese houses remain in the town.

Page 86

Phra Buddha Taksin Ming Mongkhol, Narathiwat

Located on a hill in the Khao Kong Buddhist Park, this is the tallest seated Buddha image in Thailand, 24 metres (79 feet) tall and 17 metres (56 feet) wide at the lap. It was erected in 1966.

Page 88

Wat Machi Mawat, Songkhla

Popularly called Wat Klang, this was built during the reigns of King Rama III and Rama IV though extensively restored since. Murals in the main building, dating from around a century ago, show interesting scenes of life in old Songkhla.

Page 89

Old City Wall, Nakhon Si Thammarat

One of the oldest sites in Thailand, Nakhon Si Thammarat was formerly known as Ligor and was an important city of the Srivijaya kingdom. Tradition claims that the city wall, built in the 6th century, was 2,238 metres (7,340 feet) long and 456 metres (1,496 feet) wide. Only about 100 metres (328 feet) of the wall survive today along an ancient moat.

Wat Phra Mahathat, Nakhon Si Thammarat

This is among the most sacred temples in Thailand, though its age is a matter of scholarly dispute. The main stupa, 77 metres (253 feet) tall, is in the Sri Lankan style and was erected in the early 13th century over an older Srivijaya monument. The temple complex has been extensively restored over the years.

Page 90

Central Mosque of Narathiwat

Built in 1981 in a blend of architectural styles, this is one of around 2,000 mosques in Thailand.

Page 91

Pattani Central Mosque

A trading centre since the 8th century, Pattani was once part of the Srivijaya empire. Pattani's central mosque, with its green domes and orange tiles, was built in 1963 and is Thailand's largest.

Wat Arun, the Temple of Dawn, in Bangkok.